Around Truro

IN OLD PHOTOGRAPHS

Around Truro

IN OLD PHOTOGRAPHS

Compiled by ARTHUR LYNE

From the archives of the
Royal Cornwall Museum

Alan Sutton Publishing Limited
Phoenix Mill · Far Thrupp
Stroud · Gloucestershire

First Published 1992

Copyright © Arthur Lyne 1992

British Library Cataloguing
in Publication Data

Lyne, Arthur
  Around Truro in Old Photographs
  I. Title
  942.378

  ISBN 0-7509-0175-6

Typeset in 9/10 Sabon.
Typesetting and origination by
Alan Sutton Publishing Limited.
Printed in Great Britain by
WBC Print Ltd, Bridgend.

DEDICATED
To the memory of the author's sister
RUTH LYNE
(1919–1986)
who in her youth was familiar
with the scenes in this book, as was
the author

Contents

Foreword

Growing interest in old photograpformerpast environments and lifestyles. Rapid social and scenic change surrounds us as we move ever closer to the twenty-first century, and in compiling *Around Truro in Old Photographs* from the archives of the Royal Cornwall Museum Arthur Lyne has selected material in support of a title which will generate broad appeal among those interested in the numerous facets of Cornwall's history.

That Cornwall played a prominent role in nineteenth-century photography is well known and documented; this early role provides the base upon which the Royal Institution of Cornwall has amassed its comprehensive photographic archive.

In casting the net to include villages beyond the city limits Arthur Lyne offers us a window on the townscape and landscape of Truro and its environs. A past President of both the Federation of Old Cornwall Societies and the Truro Old Cornwall Society, and holder for twenty-five years of the position of Honorary Secretary to the RIC, he is singularly well qualified to present this book.

The Royal Institution of Cornwall is pleased to participate in this publication, and we are grateful to Arthur Lyne for enabling us to share and appreciate the fascinating photographic glimpses of bygone days.

Courtenay V. Smale
President, Royal Institution of Cornwall

Introduction

The museum in River Street at Truro is owned and managed by the Royal Institution of Cornwall which was founded in 1818 and is a registered charity. The Institution has always enjoyed royal patronage, and in 1990 Her Majesty The Queen granted permission for the museum to be called the Royal Cornwall Museum instead of the County Museum, its previous name.

Apart from those six where mention is made in their captions, all the photographs in this book come from the archives of the museum and are subject to the Institution's copyright. The museum's photographic collection totals about 25,000 Cornish scenes, built up over the years by donations and including about 5,000 relating to the Truro district. With the exception of the picture of the Cathedral crypt being sandbagged the museum has no photographs of Truro during the Second World War, or at any rate none worth publishing, so donations of photographs on that subject would be welcome.

This book has been a labour of love – for the town in which I have lived all my life and for the Institution of which I have been a member for over forty years. I am very grateful for the help in the preparation of the book which I have received from the staff of the museum, especially Roger and Pat Penhallurick. The encouragement from the museum's Director, Caroline Dudley, and the guidance from the publisher's editor, Simon Thraves, are also much appreciated.

Arthur Lyne

The Old Town and Townspeople

V 222 Lemon Bridge, Truro

The River Kenwyn in about 1920, before any part of Lemon Quay car park had been made. Back Quay is on the left adjoining the back of the Municipal Buildings. Lemon Quay is on the right with the gas works in the right background. Truro College, not yet called Truro School, is on the horizon in the middle. The photograph is taken from the direction of Lemon Bridge, which stood where Lemon Street becomes Lower Lemon Street.

Covering the River Kenwyn to make the early part of Lemon Quay car park in 1926. Further covering in 1938 completed the car park.

Trap fallen off Back Quay, in 1921, before any part of Lemon Quay car park had been made. Back Quay adjoined the Municipal Buildings and the name is still used for the street there. Lemon Quay was on the opposite side of the river.

Lemon Bridge, *c.* 1920.

Lemon Quay in the early 1900s. Lemon Bridge is in the centre background. Back Quay is on the right and Lemon Quay on the left.

This photograph was taken about the same time but from the direction of Lemon Bridge.

Hicks's Garage at Boscawen Bridge in 1921. From about 1910 to the 1930s S. Hicks & Son (now at Lemon Quay) used this garage for coachwork and painting and as the depot for Fords. Another garage of theirs in the city centre was the one in Lemon Street – now the Lemon Street Market – but from 1876 right through the first half of the twentieth century their main offices and workshops were in River Street and Kenwyn Street.

Truro head post office at High Cross, *c.* 1900. This was built in 1886 on the site of the Unicorn Inn. Part of Marks & Spencer is now on the site. It was designed by Silvanus Trevail, a Truro architect who had a national reputation. Other buildings in Truro designed by him include Lloyds Bank at the corner of Boscawen Street and Lemon Street. Many public buildings throughout Cornwall are his, and at Truro and elsewhere they are often partly in red brick – a favourite material of his. He was Mayor of Truro in 1894–5. In this photograph Argall's Studio on the right of the post office was operated as a photographic business by F.E. Argall who took many of the photographs in this book. The shop marked Hendra was that of R.J. Hendra, a plumber.

Boscawen Street, *c.* 1890. The post office sign refers to a sub-post office which, according to Kelly's Directory, was in Boscawen Street in 1889. (Photograph by courtesy of Mr R.R. Martin.)

Red Lion Hotel and its annexe above Farrow's Bank, and the tailors shop of Andrew & Como, which was later Hawke's, *c.* 1910. Farrow's Bank collapsed financially in 1920 and these premises were taken over by the National Provincial Bank. That bank's premises and the hotel annexe were badly damaged by fire around 1930 and the bank moved temporarily to the building in Boscawen Street which was later Truro Savings Bank and was on the site of the Coinage Hall.

Boscawen Street, *c.* 1890. This shows Griffith's shop, which was later bought by A.W. Jordan, at No. 30 Boscawen Street. Around 1930 Mr Jordan moved to 27 Boscawen Street taking over Heard's shop there and No. 30 Boscawen Street became the *West Briton* office. Also in the picture is Gill's men's shop. Gill's drapers shop was on the opposite side of Boscawen Street where Woolworths is now. Mr Jordan was a well known photographer and many of the photographs in this book were taken by him.

Market day in Truro, *c.* 1910. The vehicles are horse buses from other towns and villages, though the residents of some riverside villages, such as Ruanlanihorne, preferred to come by water. Some of the cattle being offered for sale came on foot the previous day and spent the night in fields in or near Truro. Market day was Wednesday, then as now. The building in the left foreground is the Corn Exchange, which was on part of the site of Littlewoods.

Welcome! This is Webb's drapers shop in Boscawen Street on the site of Littlewoods. The business was founded by John Webb, continued by his son Bennett Webb, and then by his grandson John Webb. The occasion for the welcome is not certain. The shop closed around 1950 after the death of the grandson in Truro's polio epidemic in 1949.

Early lorries. In September 1919 two lorries of Cornwall Transport Company are in Boscawen Street outside the Municipal Buildings.

The second Boscawen Bridge. The first Boscawen Bridge was opened in July 1849. Some of the town's merchants having persuaded the Admiralty that a stone structure would impede navigation above it, a curved wooden bridge was built. That first bridge was unsatisfactory and this photograph (probably taken around 1900) shows the second bridge, which was opened in November 1862. This lasted until it was replaced by the present bridge in the 1960s – when the A39 ring road, now called Morlaix Avenue, was made.

The second Boscawen Bridge, photographed in the late 1930s. The large building on the right belonged to Farm Industries Ltd. On the left the building with a signboard on its front is the Britannia Hotel. The buses are outside the bus office which was in the Public Rooms, the building that included the Palace cinema.

River Street, *c.* 1900. The building in the left foreground, then Truro Savings Bank, was opened in 1919 as the Museum of the Royal Institution of Cornwall. The next building was the Baptist chapel, now the museum extension, and the spires in the background belonged to the Congregational chapel. This was later adapted for use as the offices of Truro Rural District Council.

Truro Fair on The Green, *c.* 1910.

Captain Rowland's Moving Pictures at Truro Whitsun Fair on The Green, 1910. The Moving Pictures probably constituted the first cinematographic show ever seen in Truro, preceding the opening of the cinema at the City Hall in 1912. The fairground organ is on the left.

Truro Art School, *c*. 1923. This was part of the Technical School in Union Place.

Cornwall County Council's Dairy (Travelling) School at Truro. Under Miss A.J. Nicholls the school was a prize-winner at the Crystal Palace Dairy Show and at the Royal Cornwall Show.

2028

Dame Margaret Lloyd George at Truro. The Prime Minister's wife, sitting, is being welcomed by Mr E.J. Lodge on 12 July 1922. This was in Boscawen Street. Mr N.B. Bullen, the mayor, is in the back row, third from the left.

Ben Little of Truro. This is a photograph in the Royal Institution of Cornwall's Journal for 1933–4, and the caption says: 'He is 87 years old and has toured parts of Cornwall singing wassail-songs for 73 years. The bowl of apple-wood here shown has been carried by him for over 62 years.' Wassailing was a Twelfth Night custom but the Journal concluded that 'wassailing has ceased to be alive'. Ben Little in his later years was demonstrating a custom of the past.

The six-sided pillar box at the junction of Prince's Street with Quay Street. Formerly this was thought to be one of the type designed by Anthony Trollope when he was an official of the Post Office. It was he who invented the first ever pillar box, erected in Jersey in 1852 and still used. In fact the pillar box shown is one of the Penfold boxes, dating from 1866 to 1878, so it is well over 100 years old. It is still in use.

Beare's wine and spirit store in Quay Street, during the First World War.

Truro Municipal Buildings (erected 1846–7) immediately after the fire there on 11 November 1914. The clock framework crashed down into the council chamber. An anonymous donor presented a new clock to the town.

Lower Lemon Street during the fire in Ben Carter's chemists shop, 10 November 1923.

New Bridge Street during the fire there on Sunday 11 April 1926. This fire rendered twenty-two people homeless.

Captain H.W. ('Puffer') Hockin, a Truro solicitor who was captain (that is, in command) of Truro Fire Brigade 1886–1926. In 1912 he was one of a delegation of six from the British Fire Prevention Committee to attend an International Fire Congress in St Petersburg at the invitation of the Imperial Russian Fire Service Society. In 1922 Hockin was created a freeman of the City of Truro, only the seventh on that roll. His nickname arose from his habit of blowing out his cheeks when striving for a word, because he stammered. Hockin died in 1929 aged 81, only three years after his retirement from commanding the fire brigade, although he had retired from his profession in 1913.

Making Hendra Road in the early 1920s.

Truro Borough Police Force, c. 1870. Left to right: Superintendent Woolcock, Sergeant Roberts, Constables Coad, Collett, Scown and Bettison. The force started in 1839, and later had headquarters in the Municipal Buildings (approximately where Clara Reid and The Terrace Coffee House are now). Truro police station remained there until the amalgamation of Truro City Police with the County Constabulary in 1921. At Truro in the early years of the present century a common warning of a parent to a misbehaving child was 'I'll have you under the clock'.

Truro Police Force, c. 1890 under Superintendent Angel. The town crier (white-bearded John Odgers) was considered part of the police establishment.

The Admiral Boscawen at the corner of Malpas Road and Boscawen Bridge Road (now part of Morlaix Avenue). This was closed for demolition in 1966, when the A39 ring road was made. The name was transferred to an inn in Richmond Hill. Edward Boscawen (1711–60) was a famous admiral who, during his lifetime, was nicknamed 'Old Dreadnought'. (Photograph by courtesy of Mr R.R. Martin.)

The Lord Nelson was in St Austell Street. It was demolished in the 1960s when the road was widened, at the time the Trafalgar roundabout was made. It had been a public house since 1841, and until the 1950s its name was the Union Hotel. (Photograph by courtesy of Mr R.R. Martin.)

The stack of Truro Smelting Works as seen from Malpas Road, *c.* 1895. These works were established in 1816 and closed in 1871; the stack was still standing over twenty years later.

Photographed in 1934, these are the buildings and yard off Tregolls Road which were formerly used as Truro Smelting Works. They adjoined the back of the Union Hotel, which fronted on to St Austell Street.

The Duke of Cornwall's Light Infantry on parade in High Cross in 1905.

The Armoury in Pydar Street in the 1930s. This was the headquarters of the 4th/5th Battalion of the Duke of Cornwall's Light Infantry, a battalion which was part of the Territorial Army.

Pydar Street, *c.* 1955, showing Brick House and part of the London Inn, both since demolished.

Pydar Street in May 1966. Jollief was a house decorator and Julian was a butcher.

Moresk Mill and Ford, probably in the 1870s.

St Mary's Workhouse was near Moresk Bridge and was the workhouse for the parish of St Mary from 1781 until around 1850, when Truro Poor Law Union Workhouse was opened. This was at what soon became known as Union Hill, now the upper part of Tregolls Road.

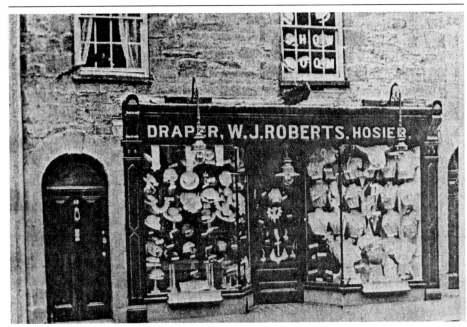

W.J. Roberts's shop in 1914. Mr Roberts had opened his first shop in St Nicholas Street in 1903. His grandson, Mr Bill Roberts, is now managing director of the large and prestigious shop in Boscawen Street.

Kenwyn Street sub-post office, kept during the 1930s and 1940s by Mr and Mrs Dunstan. They lost their only son during the Second World War, when he was serving with the Royal Air Force.

Pearson's Jewellery shop at No. 17 Boscawen Street, before 1913. Part of Littlewoods is now on the site. Pearson's shop moved to Lemon Quay around 1950 and closed in about 1970.

Rowe's grocery shop at No. 83 Lemon Street, *c.* 1903. This adjoined the Royal Hotel. The Jaeger shop is here now.

Truro Isolation Hospital, 1920. This shows Mr and Mrs Scoble, who were then in charge, and also a nurse and a patient. The hospital was near Moresk Bridge.

The Red Lion Hotel – guests arriving in style on 17 June 1905. This was built in 1671, later became 'Mr Foote's great house', and was opened as the Red Lion Inn in 1769, when the name and business moved from two doors away. It became Truro's leading hotel, and in the present century was often spoken of as the centre of the town's social life.

Interior of the Red Lion Hotel.

Staircase of the Red Lion Hotel. When the hotel was demolished, this staircase was taken to Godolphin House near Helston.

Red Lion Hotel – front exterior.

The Red Lion's last day. On the morning of 14 July 1967 a lorry came down Lemon Street and crashed into the Red Lion Hotel when its brakes failed. This caused so much damage that the building had to be pulled down. Truronians who saw this scene remember it as one of Truro's saddest days.

Prince's Street, *c.* 1880. In the foreground is the building which was used as the Miners' Bank from 1771, when that bank started, until 1808. It moved in that year to another building in the same street, which in the present century became the offices of the solicitors Coulter Hancock & Co. That has now been demolished and has been replaced by the Trustee Savings Bank.

The Old Mansion House in Quay Street, c. 1920. This was built as the town house of Samuel Enys, of Enys near Penryn, in around 1707. The Palace cinema is in the left foreground. In the left background is Blackford's Royal Printeries, now replaced by the Royal Bank of Scotland. After becoming dilapidated the Old Mansion House has recently been refurbished, this refurbishment winning an award.

West End Drapery Stores in 1911, now The Old Ale House.

The old museum, Union Place. The museum of the Royal Institution of Cornwall was here from 1834 until the transfer to the museum in River Street, which was formally opened in 1919. Part of Marks & Spencer is now on the site.

The Coinage Hall in Boscawen Street, where tin was tested and taxed. The term 'coinage' has nothing to do with the minting of coins but comes from the French *coin*, a corner. This was because the quality of the tin was judged by a small piece which was cut from a corner of the block of tin by the assay master. Truro was one of Cornwall's four coinage towns, the others being Liskeard, Lostwithiel and Helston. The coinage hall shown was pulled down in 1848 and replaced by Tweedy's Bank, followed by the Capital & Counties Bank, the National Provincial Bank (briefly, after a fire at its premises) and Truro Savings Bank. A tablet on the present building records that on 27 August 1776 and other occasions John Wesley preached here, either inside or outside the Hall.

Land Girls in Prince's Street during the First World War, *c.* 1917. They belonged to a group which was based at Tregavethan.

Logs on the Town Quay, *c.* 1920. The building in the right foreground was the monumental mason's works of Trevail, which later moved to Old Bridge Street. They are now on part of the site of Carvedras Smelting Works.

Quay Street at its junction with Duke Street (on the left), St Mary's Street (middle background) and New Bridge Street (on the right). The building on the left is Treleaven's Restaurant, one of Truro's best known restaurants until the middle of the present century. It fronted on to Prince's Street.

The Assembly Rooms at High Cross. Built in 1772, this was the venue for balls and other social events in the late eighteenth and nineteenth centuries, and also included a theatre. High Cross is named after a cross which was here in the thirteenth century and was probably the one that was re-erected here in 1988. The theatre existed until the early years of the present century. This photograph was taken around 1930 and shows the tea shop which was here then. Cathedral Garage was in the yard at the back of the building.

St Mary's Street in the 1920s. Opie's photographic shop is on the right in the foreground with the Cathedral in the background.

The Custom House in Green Street. It ceased to be used as the custom house in 1882, when the port of Truro was demoted to a creek for custom purposes. Until then the royal arms were over the door.

Truro Gas Works near Lemon Quay in the early 1950s, before the gas works were opened at Newham in 1955. There was a gas works on Lemon Quay as early as 1810, among the very first in Britain and therefore in the world. By 1822 there was gas lighting in some of the streets of Truro. The discovery of North Sea gas and the construction of a nationwide distribution system made gas works obsolete, and the Newham works were closed after only a few years of life.

Scouts being inspected by the chief scout, Lord Baden Powell, on 2 September 1919.

King Street, *c.* 1920. The tailors shop is that of John Osborn.

Lander Centenary. This is the ceremony in 1934 to commemorate the 100th anniversary of the death of Richard Lander, the Truronian who traced the course and discovered the mouths of the River Niger. The ceremony was held at the monument dedicated to him which stands at the top of Lemon Street. Trelander and Richard Lander School at Highertown were both named in his memory, and in Green Street there is a tablet marking his birthplace. In this photograph the mayor (Mr F.R. Pascoe) is on the right of the two mace-bearers.

Unveiling the war memorial. The unveiling was by the Lord Lieutenant (Mr J.C. Williams of Caerhays Castle) on 15 October 1922, and the mayor at this time was Mr N.B. Bullen. The ceremony included a service conducted by the mayor's chaplain (Canon Trevor Lewis, Sub-Dean of Truro Cathedral), the Archdeacon of Cornwall (Canon S.R. Raffles-Flint), the Revd. E.E. Bennetts (United Methodists) and the Revd J. Dunk (Wesleyan). At this time Canon Lewis was well known for his eloquent preaching which attracted large congregations.

Motor bicycles in High Cross on 24 June 1921, gathering for the district Motor Bicycle and Light Car Club's run to the Lizard.

Major A.W. Gill's car, after being destroyed by fire at Liskey Hill, Perranporth on 24 June 1906.

Major A.W. Gill's car, AF 241. The driver is Major Gill, and behind him is possibly George Powell, the dentist. Also in the back seat is A.W. Jordan, and beside Major Gill is Matthew Clemens. This car was a 15 hp Humber, which was licensed to Major Gill on 7 February 1907 – so he probably acquired it to replace the car lost by fire. The car's licence was transferred to Hicks's Garage on 15 June 1911, so this photograph would have been taken between 1907 and 1911.

Gill's staff outing to Tintagel and Boscastle on 24 June 1921. Gill & Son's drapery shop was on the site of Woolworths. Towards the end of the last century Gill's also had a men's shop on the opposite side of Boscawen Street, but that had closed long before this photograph was taken. At this time the proprietor was Major A.W. Gill, who was well known as an amateur musician and for his philanthropy to music in Cornwall. One of his hobbies was making films, and several of those which he made in the 1930s are now in the archives of the Royal Cornwall Museum, including *The Spirit of Cornwall*. Extracts from this were shown on BBC television in 1991.

Truro Knitting Mills Ltd's outing to the Festival of Britain on 30 June 1951. Knitting Mills Ltd was a private company owned, or mainly owned, by the Tonkin family of Truro. The factory was at High Cross and later at Highertown. The trade name of its products was 'fascinese'. (Photograph by courtesy of Mr R.R. Martin.)

The mayor, Mr N.B. Bullen, laying the foundation stone of the first of the Kenwyn Road council houses in 1921. He was the manager of the Truro branch of Harvey & Co., the timber merchants, and was known as 'Nat'.

Truro cattle market at Castle Hill, *c.* 1920. The site of the Norman Castle, it has now been replaced by the Law Courts, which opened in 1988.

Williams's almshouses in Pydar Street. This charity was founded in 1631 by Henry Williams, a woollen draper of Truro. The picture shows the courtyard shortly before 1890, when Theophilus Dorrington, a jeweller, rebuilt the houses and added six rooms. Other benefactions that he made are mentioned on pp. 141 and 142.

In Malpas Road in the early 1900s, below The Parade which was built in the mid-1800s. This terrace was the boyhood home of Bishop Hunkin. Other well known Truronians who lived here include 'Nat' Bullen, who appears in several photographs in this book, and Christine Oates, the artist.

Gooding's shop in 1925. This was No. 11 High Cross.

Advertising the Assembly Rooms theatre in 1840.

Truro fire brigade outside the west front of the Cathedral, still being built in around 1900.

Jennings's grocery shop in Victoria Square, decorated for the Coronation of King George V in 1911.

Boscawen Street, *c.* 1914, probably photographed from the roof of Barclays Bank. The car in the middle of the street is believed to be a Crossley 1913, a type which was used as a staff car for the British Army throughout the First World War.

Horse-drawn cabs in Boscawen Street, probably *c.* 1920.

Carnival procession at St George's Road in the early 1900s. In the foreground are the horse and cart of A.D. Brewer & Son of Truro.

Victoria Square flooded in 1955. There were even worse floods on 27 January 1988 and 11 October 1988. All these floods were created by the River Kenwyn, which flows under the square. The square used to cover the West Bridge, the structure of which remained underneath until recent flood prevention work. It is hoped that the dam which was completed at New Mill (upstream from St George's Road and Coosebean) in 1990 will prevent any repetition of these scenes.

The bottom of Mitchell Hill in 1927, showing the George and Dragon which was demolished in 1931, and the Hope which was demolished in around 1963. When advertised for sale in 1885, the George and Dragon was described as having a ten-stalled stable for twenty horses and over the stable a room to seat sixty. Its sign on a stone plaque is now in the Royal Cornwall Museum. From the rating books, the Hope would appear to have been here in the 1830s.

Truro from Kenwyn, *c.* 1870, showing Brunel's wooden viaducts and the spire of St Mary's church. At the top on the far right is the Royal Cornwall Infirmary, which opened in 1799 and is now called the City Hospital.

After the death in 1761 of Samuel Walker, the famous curate of St Mary's church, his congregation, not approving of his successor's type of services, used this building in the Leats as a chapel. That was from around 1768 to 1775, and it was called the Octagon chapel. The building was photographed in around 1879. It had been used as a cockpit before it was used as a chapel!

Truro skating rink café, *c.* 1910. Indoor skating was a popular pastime in Truro at this time. The county rink was in the Municipal Buildings.

Unionist fête at Tregolls in 1921. This is the baby show!

The mill pool on the River Allen, behind the Barley Sheaf. The mill was the Manor Mill (at the time of this photograph long since demolished) and was near East Bridge. This was where the bridge in Old Bridge Street is now. The elephant had probably been taken there from a circus for a wash.

New Bridge, seen here from Old Bridge, was built in 1775. Until then the way into Truro from east Cornwall had been via the East Bridge, since renamed Old Bridge.

The corner of Richmond Hill and Bosvigo Road. The principal business of this firm was monumental masonry. Kelly's Directory of 1914 includes the firm but subsequent directories omit it.

Lemon Street *c.* 1890, before the fire at John Julian's property in 1893.

Building the Plaza cinema in Lemon Street on 14 July 1935. A 20-ton girder is being taken to the cinema in the course of its construction.

Strangways Terrace in 1910. This terrace was built in 1836 on the site of the barracks (a tarred wooden building) which existed from 1804 to 1834 and is commemorated by the road at the back of the terrace – Barrack Lane. The terrace was built on land belonging to the Lemon family of Carclew, and was named after Lady Charlotte Fox-Strangways, a daughter of the Earl of Ilchester who married Sir Charles Lemon. Towards the end of the last century Truro College and Truro High School both started in this terrace. In the present century the Misses Dudley had a private school here. The Girls' County School, before moving to Treyew Road, was on the site of Vivian Court, between Strangways Terrace and Strangways Villas.

Boscawen Street, *c.* 1860. The Municipal Buildings are visible, having been built in 1846–7. Neither the building which became Lloyds Bank nor the building which became Barclays Bank has yet been erected. This picture dates from about sixty years after the demolition of Middle Row, which consisted of shops and houses in the centre of what became Boscawen Street.

Carvedras Smelting Works, *c.* 1870. This opened around 1750, and the Daubuz family of Killiow had the major interest from 1783 until it was closed in 1898. In the right background is Brunel's wooden viaduct (1859) which was replaced by the present viaduct in 1904. To the left is St George's (Anglican) church, which was built in 1855.

The workforce of Carvedras Smelting Works shortly before the 1898 closure. The man with the white beard is James Seymour, whom the census of 1881 recorded as living at No. 19 Richmond Terrace, aged 51. The boy kneeling on the right is John Penrose. In 1981 he was still alive and living in America, and his sister Miss Mildred Penrose was living at St Dominic Street, aged 94.

Truro from Poltisco, *c.* 1890. Brunel's wooden viaduct is in the background. The cathedral is being constructed. Ships are in the River Kenwyn between Lemon Quay on the left and Back Quay on the right, and Lemon Bridge can be seen at the end of these two quays.

St Nicholas Street from Victoria Square in 1897. Jennings, in the left foreground, were grocers who traded here for three generations. The business was founded by Amos Jennings and continued under his son John and his grandson Willy.

An airship over Truro. This photograph was taken by A.W. Jordan in January or February 1914. The earliest practical British airship was designed and constructed by Ernest Willows in 1905, and Britain's first military airship, Dirigible Number 1, flew for the first time on 10 September 1907. The length of these airships were respectively 74 ft and 84 ft, and judging from this airship it was probably one of these two types. The building in the right foreground is Gill's drapery shop; the building in the right background is the former Miners' Bank; and the building on the left is the Capital and Counties Bank, on the site of the Coinage Hall.

Boscawen Street decorated for the Bath & West Show. This show was at Truro for five days in May 1913, fifty-two years since it had last been held in Truro, and forty-five years since it had been held in Cornwall.

Truro Steam Laundry at Moresk, in the early 1900s.

Tom Blamey's car at Tregony, *c*. 1906. Mr Blamey was an estate agent and his office was at the Old Mansion House in Quay Street. He lived at Veryan.

SECTION TWO

The Vicinity

Highertown in 1913. This was about twenty years before the start of the development that has transformed the Highertown area, but most of the cottages seen here have remained, although much altered.

Chacewater, *c.* 1905.

Calenick Mill, seen here *c.* 1900, is the building on the right. The road leads to Calenick from the bottom of Arch Hill. The old smelting works is behind the trees on the left. Calenick Mill was a grist mill of the Manor of Newham and is documented as long ago as 1577. The building shown here was erected on or near the site of its predecessors in around 1830, and continued in use until a little after 1910, the last miller being John Mutton. It is now a private house.

A thatched cottage at the foot of School Hill, Calenick, which was demolished in around 1925.

Calenick Smelting Works in the late 1870s. Opening here in 1710, having been moved from Newham, the works was owned by the Lemon and Daniell families and then by the Michells and Bolithos. The works was closed in 1891 but the manager's house with its clock tower remains.

Calenick Bridge and boys playing marbles, c. 1900. The old smelting works is in the background.

The toll house at Playing Place in 1968, since demolished.

Old Kea, *c*. 1900. This is at the head of a creek of the Truro River just below Malpas. According to legend it was here that St Kea landed at the end of his voyage from Ireland. The first Kea church was here, largely dating from the fifteenth century. In 1802 the second Kea church was built near Killiow, and the body of the first church was pulled down in the following year. The tower, shown here, remained.

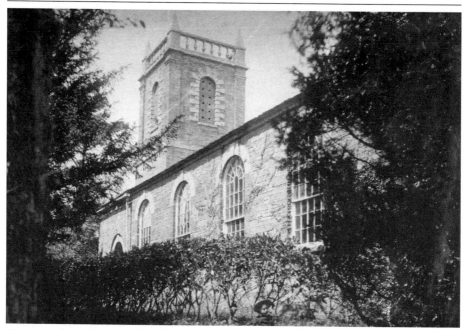

The second of the three Kea churches, seen shortly before 1895 when it was pulled down. The present Kea church is on approximately the same site.

The third Kea church, *c.* 1900.

Quaker Meeting House, at Come-to-Good in Feock parish. This was built in 1710 and is still used for Quaker meetings.

Tullimaar, Perranarworthal, built in 1829 and seen here in 1967. It was here that Kilvert the diarist spent his Cornish holiday in 1870, his host being William Hockin, a cousin of 'Puffer' Hockin (see p. 30). During the Second World War General Eisenhower visited while reviewing American troops, shortly before D-Day in 1944. After the war Tullimaar was for some years the home of Princess Bibesco.

Perran Foundry and the Norway Inn at Perranwharf in Perranarworthal parish, *c.* 1850. Perran Foundry, opened in 1791, made the heavy castings for the famous Cornish beam engines that were used for pumping water from mines, first in Cornwall and eventually all over the world. The foundry employed a large number of men and attracted subsidiary industries, such as timber yards. The Norway Inn was built in 1829, the road on which it stood having been made in 1828. At that time the river was much deeper here than it is now, and it was possible for small sailing vessels to discharge their cargoes at Perranwharf. The inn almost certainly took its name from the Norwegian ships that brought timber to Perranwharf for the mines.

Norway Hotel, *c.* 1910, with Criddle & Smith's van in front. The inn has become a hotel. Criddle & Smith, a family firm which operated in King Street and St Nicholas Street in Truro, was one of the most prestigious businesses in Cornwall.

Machinery at Great Wheal Busy near Chacewater in the early 1900s. On the back of the photograph there is a note by the late A.K. Hamilton Jenkin, the mining historian, reading, 'Perhaps the last horse whim in use in Cornwall'. Great Wheal Busy is one of the oldest copper mines in the county and was worked at various times from 1700 to the early 1900s. In its later years it also produced tin.

Killifreth Mine near Chacewater, c. 1900. It was last worked in the thirty years before 1908 for tin. In 1912 and again in 1919 there were brief and unsuccessful attempts to reopen the mine.

On the way to Idless, before 1915. The cottage is still here, between Daubuz Moors and Killagordon. The watercourse was the leat of Moresk Mill, at the other end of Daubuz Moors.

Scawswater Mill, on the River Allen near Idless. In the early nineteenth century the mill was part of the large woollen cloth industry built up by the Plummer family. It was particularly noted for its swanskin cloth, but at other times it was used for grinding corn.

The toll house at the top of Tregolls Road opposite St Clement Hospital. This was probably built in 1826 when the turnpike road from Truro to Tresillian via Woodcock Corner was opened. Before this date the way from Truro to Tresillian was up St Clements Hill and via Kiggon. The toll house was demolished in around 1965.

Truro Royal Naval Hospital during the First World War. Built in 1846–7, it was used as the workhouse for Truro Poor Law Union (which comprised twenty-four parishes including St Mary, Kenwyn and St Clement) before and after the war. It was commonly known as 'the Union' and the road outside was Union Hill. It is now St Clement Hospital.

Ward X of Truro Royal Naval Hospital, which was in a wooden extension. After the First World War it was taken to Ladock, where it is now the village hall.

Hospital Christmas, either 1917 or 1918, at Truro Royal Naval Hospital.

Pencalenick House from the south-west, probably in the 1890s. It was built in 1883 by Michael Henry Williams, a cousin of the Williams families at Scorrier and Caerhays Castle, and the architect was J.P. St Aubyn. A small Georgian house here, home of the Vivian family, was demolished before this house was built. Michael Henry Williams lived here from 1883 until his death in 1902, and was succeeded by his son Henry Harcourt Williams who lived here until 1915. Because of the war he went to his smaller house at nearby Penair, and never returned. His son Francis Williams sold the house in around 1948 to Cornwall County Council, which runs it as a special school.

Kiggon Pond near Tresillian, *c.* 1900. This was dammed off from the Tresillian River in the late 1820s by John Vivian, then owner of Pencalenick, so as to form a lake in the grounds of his house. In 1853, though, when his widow was preparing to sell Pencalenick, it was discovered that the bed of the pond, being foreshore, was the property of the Duchy of Cornwall. In order to keep the pond as part of Pencalenick she had to buy the foreshore from the Duchy.

St Clement Churchtown, *c.* 1910. The middle of the three cottages on the left was the Ship Inn from about 1844 until 1908. To the right of these cottages is the lychgate with a room over it. The church dates from the fourteenth century, but has had many subsequent alterations ('restorations'). It was the church of the Duchy manor of Moresk.

The Ignioc Stone, now outside the south wall of St Clement's church, is thought to date from *c*. AD 500. When the antiquarian William Borlase saw it in 1754 it was serving as a gatepost of St Clement's Vicarage. The stone was scheduled as a National Monument in 1932 and was set up in its present position in 1938. The stone gets its name from the word *Ignioc*, inscribed around AD 600 about fifty years after the earlier inscription – *Vital Fili Torrici*. These inscriptions are thought to be memorials to two different persons. The photograph on the left shows the stone being set up in its present position, while the other picture shows it in its previous position, in the garden of St Clement's Vicarage.

Tresillian Bridge, *c.* 1904, the year the church was consecrated and before the Sunday School (now adjoining) was built. An artist with an easel can be seen. The bridge is a modern structure, but there was a bridge here as early as 1309. On 10 March 1646, on or near this spot, a parley took place between the defeated Royalist army under Hopton (based at Truro) and the victorious Roundheads under Fairfax (based at Tregony). The resulting treaty was signed at Truro two days later and virtually put an end to the Civil War.

Merther church near Tresillian, *c*. 1900. It dates from the 1300s but is now ruinous. In 1904 a church was built at Tresillian Bridge, and to that were removed the font, bells and pulpit. Charles Henderson in his *Cornish Church Guide*, published in 1925, said 'Merther is now only used for mortuary purposes. It is a building of great interest and it is much to be regretted that no timely repairs seem to be forthcoming.' There is a churchyard but that too is dilapidated, and there have been no burials there in recent years.

Tresawsan, in Merther parish. The photograph was probably taken on the visit of Truro Old Cornwall Society on 26 July 1924. Tresawsan was the home of the Hals family for many generations, and the historian William Hals was born here in 1655.

Golden Manor in the parish of Probus, photographed in 1935. The back part of the house is Tudor (1530s) and it was there that Cuthbert Mayne (canonized in 1970) was arrested in 1577. He was executed at Launceston, a victim of the penal laws against Roman Catholics imposed by the Elizabethan government after the Pope had claimed to depose Queen Elizabeth and called on her Catholic subjects to rebel.

The medieval mansion at Golden which was the forerunner of the Tudor house. This photograph was taken in 1935.

Tregony Bridge, from a postcard sent 28 September 1909. A bridge had been here since the 1300s. The river is the Fal, which was tidal here in the Middle Ages, so that in the reign of King John Tregony was a more important port than Truro. Tregony sent two members to Parliament from 1294 until the Reform Act of 1832.

Tregony almshouses in the early 1900s. This was originally a charity for 'six decayed housekeepers' founded by Hugh Boscawen in 1696. The building was restored in around 1897.

The first motor car in Tregony. Mr Edgar Lidgey outside Cuby House in 1914.

Golden Vale Dairy, Probus, probably in the 1920s. Kelly's Directory lists Golden Vale Dairy Society Ltd at Parkengear, Probus.

Probus School in 1925. This school functioned from 1853 to 1960. Founded by the Revd D. Trinder, then curate of Probus parish church, it was a private boarding school and had a high reputation. The building shown in this photograph was designed by the famous architect G.E. Street, who supervised its construction; it was opened in 1860.

Probus church tower in the early 1900s. This is the highest tower of any parish church in Cornwall and is also claimed to be the finest in the county. On the site of a monastic foundation in Celtic days, the present church building dates from the fifteenth century. At one time the parish of Probus was so rich and extensive that its tithe supported a dean, five prebendaries, a vicar and two chaplains!

Probus Square in the early 1900s. On the right is the Hawkins Arms, named after the Hawkins family of nearby Trewithen.

On a country walk. This shows the clothes (especially the ladies' hats) considered suitable for a walk in the countryside near Truro in about 1900. On the extreme right is the author's mother.

St Erme church in the early 1900s. This was rebuilt in 1820 except for the tower, which dates from the fifteenth century. Inside there is a memorial to Cornelius Cardew who was master of Truro Grammar School from 1771 to 1805. He was also rector of St Erme and at the same time rector of Lelant, which in his time included St Ives.

This shows the scene after a fire at St Erme on 6 June 1908. The fire had been caused by a spark from the chimney which ignited the thatched roof. The *Royal Cornwall Gazette* of 11 June reported how the fire was dealt with by Truro Fire Brigade: 'Mr W. Hitchens had the engines horsed in smart time and covered the distance expeditiously . . . Captain Hockin started later in a motor and arrived as soon as the brigade, thus demonstrating the value and necessity of an engine driven by motor power.'

The Wheel Inn at Tresillian in the early 1900s. This inn uses a ship's wheel for a sign, which is appropriate since the house is on the riverside. The recorded names of the landlords go back to 1770.

Zelah village, c. 1910. The Hawkins Arms is on the right, named after the Hawkins family of Trewithen who were, and whose descendants still are, large landowners in the locality.

Zelah, *c.* 1910, showing crowds with horses and traps on their way to Summercourt Fair.

Summercourt Fair, the destination of the crowds shown in Zelah. The Michaelmas fair is held on 25 September each year and dates back to the Middle Ages, being documented as long ago as the reign of King Edward II.

Trispen, *c.* 1900. The building on the left is the Reading Room which was established in 1884. The printed words 'St Erme', are incorrect, although Trispen is in the parish of St Erme.

Trispen in the early 1900s – not 'St Erme Village'. On the right is the post office and beyond that the White Hart Inn, under Lipton's sign advertising tea.

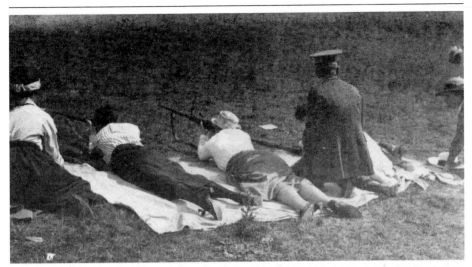

Ladies' shooting competition. From Monday 11 August 1919 to the following Friday 15 August the 12th Volunteer Battalion of the Duke of Cornwall's Light Infantry had a rifle shooting meeting at Idless. This photograph shows women competing.

The top prize-winner in the Ladies' Shooting Competition at Idless – Miss C.A. Oliver.

Trehane south front in 1935. This was a Queen Anne mansion in Probus parish, about a mile north from Tresillian. In September 1946 it was reduced to a shell by a disastrous fire and has never been rebuilt. The present owner has converted the stable into a dwelling house, and lives there adjoining the well known gardens.

Truro water works below Woodcock Corner in April 1970.

SECTION THREE

The Cathedral

St Mary's church shortly before its demolition to make way for the Cathedral, the building of which started in 1880. The south aisle of this church was saved from demolition and incorporated in the Cathedral as St Mary's aisle, used as parish church for the city centre. The Cathedral nave now occupies the site of the churchyard and gates shown in this photograph.

The foundation stones ceremony on 20 May 1880. This photograph shows the Prince of Wales, the future King Edward VII, laying the memorial stone in the projected nave. He had just laid the main foundation stone at the north-east corner of what became the choir.

Building the Cathedral. The workforce around 1883.

The Cathedral's west front, completed
to above the west door. The vehicles
are horse buses parked in High
Cross, which was the departure
point for other towns and villages.

The Cathedral, *c.* 1909, showing the western towers in scaffolding. They were completed in 1910.

A steeplejack on a Cathedral spire. The date is not known but the photograph was probably taken about the time of completion.

Bishop Frere at his enthronement, on 20 November 1923. A member of the (Anglican) Order of the Community of the Resurrection at Mirfield, he was the first monk to be appointed a bishop in the Church of England since the Reformation, and there was much opposition in Cornwall to his appointment. However, by the time of his retirement twelve years later he had endeared himself to the Cornish people, and is remembered as a saintly man and a lover of music.

Bishop Hunkin at his enthronement in the Cathedral on 25 June 1935. The son of a Truro coal merchant, he was 'our own Cornish bishop' until his sudden death in 1950. During the First World War he served in Gallipoli and in the trenches in France, and his bravery earned him the MC and Bar. On Hunkin's memorial tablet in the Cathedral the inscription says he was 'a man greatly beloved'. This was certainly true.

This shows boys of Truro Cathedral School in October 1939, filling and stacking sand-bags around the crypt of the Cathedral. According to Mr Stanley Mischler, headmaster, when the sandbags were removed at the end of the war a honeycomb was discovered behind some of them.

SECTION FOUR

Royal Visits

Triumphal arches erected in Truro when the foundation stones of the Cathedral were laid by the Prince of Wales, the future King Edward VII, on 20 May 1880. The arches were all designed by Silvanus Trevail, the Truro architect who is mentioned several times elsewhere in this book.

The young princes outside the Cathedral. These were Edward (aged 16), the future King Edward VIII, and Albert (aged 15), the future King George VI, on a private visit in 1911 while convalescing after measles. When opening the new museum at Truro eight years later, the elder prince recalled that in 1911 he had visited the old museum, because 'I thought I should make a very poor Duke of Cornwall if I did not know the difference between tin and wolfram.'

Ellen Jane Treglown on the left and Blanche Paull on the right, chambermaids at Southleigh in Lemon Street. The future King Edward VII visited Southleigh on 20 May 1880 to put on masonic regalia before processing to the Cathedral site.

119

The Prince and Princess of Wales, the future King George V and Queen Mary, in Richmond Hill on 15 July 1903. They had come to Truro to be present at the service in the Cathedral for the Benediction of the Nave. They were staying at Tregothnan, and after the service and the luncheon in the Municipal Buildings they started their return to Tregothnan with a drive around Truro. This took them along Lemon Street, Daniell Street, Treyew Road, past the railway station and down Richmond Hill to River Street and Boscawen Street.

Royal garden party. This shows the Prince and Princess of Wales during their visit to Cornwall in July 1903. The garden party was probably at Tregothnan, where they spent several nights and where there was a house party. (Photograph by courtesy of Mr R.R. Martin.)

The Prince of Wales, the future King Edward VIII and Duke of Windsor, on 11 June 1919, inspecting a scout troop at the Royal Cornwall Show, Truro.

The Prince of Wales approaching the museum during his visit to Truro on 11 June 1919, when he opened the new Museum of the Royal Institution of Cornwall. The mayor was Mr John Tonkin and the town clerk was Mr F. Parkin. By permission of Queen Elizabeth II, given in 1990, the museum is now called the Royal Cornwall Museum. The Prince is in the uniform of a Colonel of the Duke of Cornwall's Light Infantry.

Opening the new museum. This was the platform group on 11 June 1919. In the centre is John Charles Williams of Caerhays Castle, who was the president of the Royal Institution of Cornwall and also the Lord Lieutenant. On his right is the Prince of Wales, and on his left is John Tonkin, the mayor. Behind the mayor are George Penrose, the curator of the museum, and Canon Mills, a vice-president of the Institution. Henry Jenner, the honorary secretary of the Institution, is the man in the front row with a white beard.

SECTION FIVE

Malpas
pron. Mō´ pŭs!

Malpas ferry-slip in 1912. Marjorie Burley, aged 6, is seated holding a doll.

Malpas regatta, 1909. The regatta happened to be in progress on 7 September 1846 when Queen Victoria with her husband Prince Albert and the future King Edward VII (aged 4) visited Malpas by water. The Queen and the little prince remained on board while Prince Albert went to see Truro's Municipal Buildings, then in course of construction. Victoria Point at Malpas commemorates the visit. Malpas regatta is an annual event and the residents elect a 'Mayor of Malpas' to preside.

The Park Inn and part of Trenhaile Terrace, *c.* 1925. The inn is the first building on the left and since 1962 has been called the Heron Inn. It has been a public house since 1836, and received its earlier name from the land on which it was built in around 1835. It was part of the Park estate.

The Ship Inn at Malpas in 1897. Shortly after the closure in 1852 of the Ship Inn (the larger of the two buildings in the left background) on the St Michael Penkevil side of Malpas Passage this inn with the same name was opened. It remained open until around 1921. The inn enjoyed a right of access to the shore and had its own private jetty – a considerable asset, because many of its customers arrived by water.

This is a painting of 'Jenny Mopus', who operated Malpas Ferry at the end of the eighteenth century and the beginning of the nineteenth. She used a large rowing boat, the *Happy Go Lucky*, with her real name, Jane Davis, painted on the stern. In 1804 she not only rescued Lord Falmouth's post from robbery but secured the robber. On being asked what gave her the most trouble on her ferry boat Jenny replied, 'Wemmin and Pigs'. She died in 1832 aged 82. The painting is now in the Royal Cornwall Museum.

Malpas in 1895–1900, from the St Michael Penkevil side. Cargoes for Truro were often transported by barge from here. In the right background is the shipbuilding yard of Scoble & Davies. The vessels built there included schooners and brigantines and the pleasure steamer *New Resolute*. The *Malpas Belle*, also built there, was said to be the largest ship built in the Port of Truro, and the only Truro-built vessel to round Cape Horn.

Looking downriver from Malpas, *c*. 1912. On the left is the Tresillian River and in the centre is the Truro River bending towards Truro. The woods on the right are in the parish of Kea, towards Woodbury. The two buildings on the left are in the parish of St Michael Penkevil, the larger building having been the Ship Inn from around 1774 until 1852, and the smaller building being the ferryman's cottage.

Malpas ferry about 1900. The ferry is a horse-boat similar to that used at King Harry Ferry until a steam ferry started there in 1889. The printed words 'R. Fal' are inaccurate because this is Truro River, which does not join the Fal until just above Tolverne.

To Sail the First of April,

1841,

FOR QUEBEC,

The fine fast sailing, British-built, Copper bolted BARQUE

VITTORIA,

650 Tons Burthen,

Mosey Simpson, Commander,

LYING AT MALPUS, IN TRURO RIVER,

Has very superior accommodation for Steerage and Cabin Passengers.

The Commander having been many years in the North American Trade, can give much valuable information regarding the Colonies, to any that may feel disposed to take a passage in the said ship.

Apply to the CAPTAIN on board,

Mrs. SIMPSON, at the Seven Stars Inn, Truro,

Or to the Owner, NICHOLAS MITCHELL, Malpus.

Dated, February 13th, 1841.

E. HEARD, PRINTER, BOOKBINDER, &c., BOSCAWEN-STREET, TRURO.

Emigration to Canada from Malpas! This is not so surprising as might at first be thought, because in 1841 ships were bringing timber to Malpas from Canada (and also from Norway and Sweden), so this was an opportunity to fill ships returning to Canada.

The Rivers

The River Kenwyn on the left joins the River Allen on the right to form Truro River. The topsail schooner has not been identified.

Worth's Quay, *c.* 1912. The shelter was built in 1911, and was demolished when the A39 ring road was made in the 1960s. (Photograph by courtesy of Mr R.R. Martin.)

Princess Victoria approaches Worth's Quay, *c.* 1912. She started operating in 1907. Other passenger steamers plying between Falmouth and Truro in the first forty years of the present century included the *New Resolute* and the *Queen of the Fal*. None of them continued after the outbreak of the Second World War. *Princess Victoria* and *Queen of the Fal* were both acquired by the Ministry of War Transport in 1942 and never returned. *New Resolute*, built in 1882 by Scoble & Davies of Malpas, was sold in 1927. This *Queen of the Fal* was the second of that name, replacing the first in 1912.

A Wesleyan outing assembled at Truro for a steamer voyage, probably to and from St Just or St Mawes, and probably around 1920 when such trips were very popular.

Lizzie in Truro River approaching the Town Quay with the buildings of Hosken, Trevithick, Polkinhorn & Co. in the background. This 82-ton schooner was built at Malpas by Scoble & Davies and was launched in 1881. She sailed on a regular cargo service route between Truro and London. In 1900 she was sold to Joseph Weston Hunkin of Truro, the father of the future Bishop of Truro. In 1905 *Lizzie*, while under the command of Captain Sara, became a total loss off Gravesend while *en route* for Falmouth with a cargo of manure.

Timber baulks were brought up the river from Malpas by rafts for Harvey & Co. This was still being done in the 1920s when the photograph was taken.

Queen of the Fal at Sunny Corner in 1895. This was the first pleasure steamer of that name. It was built in 1893 and operated from then, mainly between Truro and Falmouth, until it was sold in 1911 for work on the Thames. The steamer was at once replaced by the second *Queen of the Fal*. In 1865 the Prince and Princess of Wales visited Sunny Corner. They came by water, as the Prince had done with his parents in 1846, when he was 4 years old.

Woodbury House on the Truro River, just below Malpas. In the 1920s, about the time of this photograph, the pleasant custom was for boating parties to land here for tea in the garden overlooking the river. Historically, Woodbury is associated with Henry Martyn (1781–1812), the missionary to whom the baptistry in Truro Cathedral is a memorial. Born at Truro of a Truro family, he spent holidays in this house, which was the home of his brother-in-law.

This is the coaster *Erimus* leaving Devoran, *c*. 1912. She was operated by a Devon company and used in the coal trade.

LOE AND FEOCK REGATTA 1909

Feock regatta in 1909.

Beating the river bounds. Until the creation of the town of Falmouth in 1662, Truro's jurisdiction over the River Fal extended as far as Black Rock at the Fal's mouth. In the early 1700s, Truro's water bounds were pushed back to their present limits, a line between Tarra Point in Mylor parish and Messack Point in St Just parish. Since then there has been periodically (usually every six years) a ceremony of beating the bounds. This shows the ceremony on 12 July 1929. The mayor is Mr R.K. Worth; on the right is the town clerk, Mr L.J. ('Jack') Carlyon; and on the left is Mr Alfred ('Shinnery') Richards.

The ceremony of beating the bounds includes the 'arrest for a debt of £999 19s. 11³/₄d.'. In the 1923 ceremony the 'prisoner' was the mayor's chaplain, Canon Trevor Lewis, sub-dean of Truro Cathedral and rector of St Mary's. As mentioned elsewhere in this book, Canon Lewis was well known for his eloquent preaching which attracted large congregations.

The ceremony of beating the bounds also includes the re-cutting of the letters T B on the boundary stones at Tarra Point and Messack Point by the mayor, so as to maintain their legibility. In the 1929 ceremony R.K. Worth is carrying out this duty.

Warships in the Fal, soon after the end of the Second World War. Left to right: HMS *Caledon*, HMS *Albatross*, HMS *Capetown*, HMS *Adventure*, HMS *Colombo*.

Submarines in Restronguet Creek soon after the end of the Second World War. HMS *Terrapin* is on the right, HMS *Thresher* in the middle.

Mary Barrow, *c.* 1934. This three-masted topsail schooner was built at Falmouth in 1891. Originally registered in Barrow, she was later re-registered at Truro and worked out of Cornish ports. Her final skipper and part owner was Captain Peter Mortensen of Truro.

Parks, Sports and Celebrations

The Waterfall Gardens before 1904, when Brunel's wooden viaduct of 1859, shown in the photograph, was replaced by the present viaduct. These gardens were donated to the city in 1893 by Edward Goodridge Heard, mayor in 1872–3. On the site was the culver (pigeon) house of St Dominic's Friary, which was in the triangle between the present River Street and the present Kenwyn Street from the 1400s until the Dissolution of the Monasteries in the next century. As late as the nineteenth century the land was styled Culver Close, so the pigeons were still commemorated.

The mayor receiving a tank in 1920 from the War Savings Association, in recognition of war savings in Truro during the First World War. The tank was handed over to the mayor (Mr W.A. Phillips) by an officer of the Tank Corps in the Waterfall Gardens. It remained on display there until removed in the Second World War. The officer handing over the tank said he could not give the tank's battle history, but it had been to France and he understood that it had fought in the Battle of Cambrai in 1917.

Victoria Gardens, c. 1910. These gardens were laid out by Truro City Council to commemorate Queen Victoria's Diamond Jubilee on 20 June 1897. The gardens were opened on 20 June 1898. The drinking fountain on the left was given by Theophilus Dorrington to commemorate Victoria's 81st birthday on 24 May 1900 (her last, as she died in January 1901) and the gardener's lodge was given by him to commemorate the Coronation of King Edward VII in 1902. Mr Dorrington was mayor in 1884–5 and again in 1896–7, and he was made a Freeman of the City in 1903. Other benefactions by him are mentioned on pp. 59 and 142.

Victoria Gardens entrance in the early 1900s, but after 1904 because the present viaduct has been built.

Boscawen Park. Truro City Council started creating this park in around 1900, and it has been progressively extended throughout the century. The fountain on the right is inscribed, 'Presented to the Citizens of Truro by Kathleen, Viscountess Falmouth, 1907.'

Boscawen Park shelter, seen here *c.* 1910, was given by Theophilus Dorrington in 1907.

The Junket House at Boscawen Park, now Trennick Mill Restaurant. The present pond in the park was the mill pool of the former Trennick Mill. In 1854 this building was called the Mill House.

Believed to be Truro Cricket Club team, *c.* 1912. In the back row wearing a blazer is H.B. Beddall, the first ever Inland Revenue district valuer at Truro. Harry Lyne, the author's father, is on the far right of the back row. He was the district valuer at Truro from 1936 to 1944.

Skating on Tresemple Pond, alongside the riverside walk from Tresillian to St Clement Churchtown, in January or February 1917. The three sailors in the lower photograph were probably patients from Truro Royal Naval Hospital. This scene is unique because Tresemple Pond has probably never been so deeply frozen since – not even in January 1947, February 1956 or January 1987. People are shown using skates which were rarely appropriate for use out of doors in Cornwall.

Truro Bowling Club on 8 May 1914. This was the opening match of the season and was between a team captained by Isaac Roskelly, the mayor of Truro, and a team captained by W.G. Goodfellow, the previous year's mayor.

Opening Boscawen Park tennis courts in 1923 or 1924. The mayor, Mr E.J. Lodge, on behalf of the citizens, is being handed a tennis racket.

Victory tea at Hendra in 1945.

Peace celebration in 1945. This is in a field on Trehaverne Farm.

Schools

The old Grammar School in St Mary's Street, in the middle of the nineteenth century. Truro Grammar School was founded in 1549, and became Truro Cathedral School in 1906. This was the school building from the early 1700s until 1877, with a short break for improvements in 1860. Pupils here included such nationally famous Cornishmen as Edward Pellew, the eighteenth/early nineteenth-century admiral, Richard Hussey Vivian, who led the final cavalry charge at the Battle of Waterloo, and Humphry Davy, who invented the miners' safety lamp. The building is now part of the club premises of the Royal British Legion.

Interior of the old Grammar School. This is the plaque of the Arms of the Borough of Truro, with the date 1730 which hung over the master's dais in the schoolroom. The sketch was made in 1880. The plaque is now in the Royal Cornwall Museum.

St John's Sunday School at the top of Infirmary Hill. This was demolished in 1962. Truro Grammar School was housed here from 1877 to 1880, when it was moved to Tregolls House until 1891. Later it moved to Newham House, which was its home when it became Truro Cathedral School in 1906; from there it went to the new purpose-built school-house near the Cathedral in 1909. As late as the 1920s, the boys of Truro Cathedral School were called 'grammar-sows' and the boys of Truro College were called 'collie-dogs'.

Girls of Truro High School, *c.* 1917. This was taken at Trevosa (near Kenwyn church), then the school's boarding house.

Tregolls House in 1970, when it was a boarding house of Truro High School. Originally part of the Spry estate, it was at various times the home of Sir Samuel Spry, Robert Tweedy (of the Truro banking family) and the Misses Rashleigh. From 1880 to 1891 Truro Grammar School was here.

Laying the foundation stone of Truro County School for Girls on 3 October 1925. The school opened in 1927. The stone was laid by Lord Eustace Percy, President of the Board of Education. The platform party included Lady Eustace Percy, Sir Arthur Carkeet (Vice-Chairman of the County Council), Sir Arthur Quiller-Couch, Mrs Harcourt Williams (of Pencalenick), Ingeborg, Lady Molesworth-St Aubyn, the mayor and mayoress of Truro (Alderman and Mrs May), Miss Foreman (headmistress), Mrs Hext, Canon Trevor Lewis, Mr W.L. Platts (clerk of the County Council) and Mr F.R. Pascoe (clerk of the County Education Committee). Until 1927 the school was at No. 11 Strangways Terrace.

Trispen Argyle footballers in 1922. Back row, left to right: R. Chapman, S. Trethewey, E. Dark. Middle row: A. Butland, P. Brewer, H. Hocking. Front row: H. Trethewey, B. Gill, G. Wakeley, G. Trethewey, N. Harper.

Truro College war memorial pavilion opened on 18 October 1920 as memorial to the fifty-three boys of Truro College who fell in the First World War. It was in the field which now belongs to Truro Rugby Club, and was accidentally burnt down after the Second World War.

Truro School Old Boys' Association, *c*. 1947. Front row, left to right: G.L. Beards, Mr A. Lowry Creed (headmaster), L.A. Dotson (chairman), S. Mitchell, E.S. Vincent, E.T. Hawken Rowse (future Chairman of Cornwall County Council). The second row includes H.V. Guy behind Mr Creed. The third row includes J.S. Webb (extreme left) and J.N. Rosewarne (third from right). The fourth row includes S.J.D. Vage (centre) and W.A.J. Davey (Mr Vage's right). The back row includes F.G. Beale and W.C. Argall (both in front of window).

SECTION NINE

Railways

Newham railway station was Truro's first station. It was opened on 10 April 1855 as the terminus of the West Cornwall Railway line from Penzance to Truro. The mayor declared the day a public holiday and flags were hung out across the streets. At 9.30 a.m. a procession left from the Town Hall for Newham. At 11 a.m. a train arrived from Penzance carrying members of the West Cornwall Railway Company and visitors from the west of the county. In 1859, on the opening of Brunel's bridge across the Tamar, the Cornwall Railway's line from Plymouth reached Truro with its terminus at the present railway station. From 1859 to 1863 there were two passenger stations at Truro, the West Cornwall Railway's to Newham and the Cornwall Railway's at the top of Richmond Hill, but in 1863 Newham station was closed to passengers although it continued as a goods station until 1965.

The West Cornwall Railway from Penzance to Truro (opened 1855) was standard gauge, whereas the Cornwall Railway from Plymouth to Truro (opened 1859) was broad gauge. From 1866 the Cornwall Railway extended its broad gauge line from Truro to Penzance, but in May 1892 the line throughout its length from Exeter was changed to the standard gauge. The conversion was exceptionally well organized and completed in two days. About five thousand men took part, deployed at about twenty-five per mile of track. Here the changing of the gauge at Truro is shown on 21 or 22 May 1892.

The last broad gauge train to Penzance at Truro, on 20 May 1892.

The first standard gauge train, going through Truro on 23 May 1892.

Brunel's wooden viaduct shortly before it was replaced in 1904 by the present viaduct.

The new Carvedras viaduct being built. Brunel's wooden viaduct is still there, and the workmen are building the present viaduct, part of a pier of which can be seen on the left.

Female staff are pictured on a platform of Truro railway station during the First World War.

Women railway employees at Truro railway station during the First World War – around 1915.

Truro railway station in the early 1900s, before Coronation Terrace was built.

Lean's van outside Truro railway station, probably *c.* 1910. R.J. Lean operated a fleet of vans for transporting goods to and from railways. His head office was in Victoria Square, with branch offices in other towns.

Acknowledgements

Leslie Douch – for information
The late John Rosewarne – for information
Rex Hall – for research
Russell Martin – for photographs
Anthony Unwin – for research

Bibliography

Rex Barratt, *Life in Edwardian Truro*, 1977
W.J. Burley, *The City of Truro 1877–1977*
R.E. Davidson, *The History of Truro Grammar and Cathedral School*, 1970
H.L. Douch, *The Book of Truro*, 1977
A. Fairclough, *The Story of Cornwall's Railways*, 1970
F.E. Halliday, *A History of Cornwall*, 1959
Keith Hitchman, 'Newham Station Revisited', in *Truro News*
Kelly's Directory of Cornwall
Alan Kittridge, *Passage Steamers of the River Fal*, 1988
J. Meyrick, *Footsteps round St Mary's Truro*, 1987
H. Miles Brown, *The Story of Truro Cathedral*, 1991
The Norway Hotel, Perranwharf
Charles Olson, *Old Cornwall* Volume VIII, No. 12, Spring 1979
The *Royal Cornwall Gazette*
Truro Buildings Research Group, *From Moresk Road to Malpas*, 1988
Truro Buildings Research Group, *In and Around St Clement Churchtown*, 1991
Ann Weeks, *A Family Concern*, 1976
The *West Briton*